CRAFTS FOR ALL SEASONS

CREATING WITH
PAPIER-MÂCHÉ

Published by Blackbirch Press, Inc.
260 Amity Road
Woodbridge, CT 06525

©2000 by Blackbirch Press, Inc.
First Edition

Originally published as: *Disfruta con Papel Maché* by Victoria Seix, Professor of Art.

Original Copyright: ©1996 Parramón Ediciones, S.A., World Rights, Published by Parramón Ediciones, S.A., Barcelona, Spain.

e-mail: staff@blackbirch.com
Web site: www.blackbirch.com

Printed in Spain

10 9 8 7 6 5 4 3 2 1

Library of Congress Cataloging-in-Publication Data
Seix, Victoria.
[Disfruta con papel mâché. English]
Creating with papier mâché / by Victoria Seix.
    p.   cm. — (Crafts for all seasons)
Includes index.
Summary: Explains how to make and decorate various items out of papier mâché.
ISBN 1-56711-439-3 (hardcover : alk. paper)
1. Papier mâché—Juvenile literature. [1. Papier mâché. 2. Handicraft.] I. Title II. Series: Crafts for all seasons (Woodbridge, Conn.)
TT871 .S45 2000   00-008071
646.4'78—dc21   CIP
                                                          AC

Contents

✄ = *Adult supervision strongly recommended*

A Slippery Snake	4
Star Cruiser	6
Terrific Pencil Toppers	8
Mini-Houses	10
Nutty Neckties	12
Happy-Hair Headbands	13
A Ghostly Game	14
Clever Clips and Pins	16
Rovin' Robot	18
Moustache Mask	20
Funtastic Footprints	22
A House Mouse	23
Peeking Person	24
Hangers with Heart	26
Money Melon Bank ✄	28
How to Work with Paper Strips	30
How to Make Paper Pulp	31
Where to Get Supplies	32
For More Information	32
Index	32

CRAFTS FOR ALL SEASONS

CREATING WITH
PAPIER-MÂCHÉ

BLACKBIRCH PRESS, INC.
WOODBRIDGE, CONNECTICUT

A Slippery Snake

1. Bend and twist a wire, as shown.

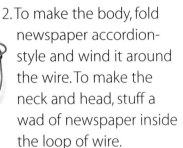

2. To make the body, fold newspaper accordion-style and wind it around the wire. To make the neck and head, stuff a wad of newspaper inside the loop of wire.

☞ *YOU'LL NEED: a long piece of wire, newspaper, masking tape, scissors, water, paints, construction paper, a paintbrush, glue, and a sponge.*

3. Wrap the snake with enough masking tape to hold the paper in place.

4. Cover the snake with strips of newspaper coated on both sides with glue. (See page 30 to learn how to prepare the strips.)

5. Apply two layers of newspaper. When the newspaper dries, paint the snake a light color.

6. Wrap masking tape around the middle of a piece of sponge to make a stamp.

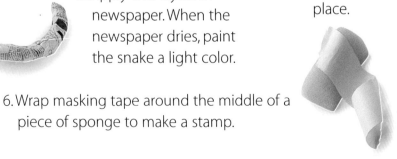

7. Soak the stamp in paint and decorate the snake's body.

8. Repeat the process using the two other stamps, each with a different color of paint.

9. Draw the snake's tongue on construction paper, cut it out, and glue it to the mouth.

10. Paint the eyes and the mouth. Watch out! It might be poisonous!

💡 *Use your imagination: What other animals can you make by using the same basic shape? How about an earthworm or an eel?*

Star Cruiser

1. Coat two same-size soup bowls with liquid soap. Line them with crisscrossed strips of moistened and glued newspaper. Remember to ask an adult before taking any dishes.

☞ **YOU'LL NEED: two same-size soup bowls, liquid soap, newspaper, glue, water, cord, paint, scissors, and fluorescent stickers.**

2. Once the newspaper dries, carefully remove the bowls.

3. Make a hole in the center of one of the paper bowls. Thread a cord through the hole, and tie a knot to secure the cord.

4. Glue the two bowls both together, as shown.

5. Cut off the excess paper around the rim.

💡 **Use your imagination:** You can use the same technique to make planets, stars, moons, and other space vehicles. For rounder planets, use a rounder bowl, and for longer shapes use a coffee mug.

6. Paint the saucer. When the paint dries, attach fluorescent stickers. Hang your star cruiser from the ceiling with the cord.

7

Terrific Pencil Toppers

☞ YOU'LL NEED:
paper pulp, glue, plastic wrap, masking tape, pencils, paints, and a paintbrush.

1. Cover part of each pencil with plastic wrap and masking tape, as shown.

2. To make a shark, place paper pulp over the eraser end of a pencil. Shape the mouth and wait until the pulp is almost dry. Then add the tail and fins. Paint the shark when it is dry. (See page 32 to learn how to make paper pulp.)

3. To make a seal, place a roll of paper pulp over the eraser end of a pencil. Bend the neck up and the tail down. When the pulp is half dry, add more pulp to the head, body, and tail. Attach the feet. Paint the seal when it is dry.

4. To make an octopus, put a ball of pulp at the end of a pencil and shape it to make the neck. When the head is half dry, add the rolls for the eight tentacles. Paint it when it is dry.

5. To make a person's face, cover the eraser end of a pencil with pulp. When the figure is half dry, add the features. To make a man, add a hat or beard. To make a woman, add hair or a hat. Paint your person when it is dry.

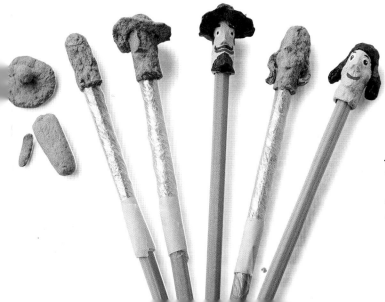

💡 **Use your imagination:** You could also make each member of your family, including pets. You could even do a collection of your best friends!

Mini-Houses

1. Coat the inside of a plastic container with liquid soap. If the lid has grooves, seal it with plastic wrap instead of liquid soap.

2. Cover the inside of the container and the outside of the lid with four layers of paper strips, placing one layer on top of the other.

☛ **YOU'LL NEED: newspaper, glue, water, cord, construction paper, plastic wrap, plastic container, liquid soap, paints, a paintbrush, a pencil, and scissors.**

3. Once the paper dries, remove the plastic container and lid.

4. Cut off the excess paper from the base and the lid.

5. Glue the base and lid together.

6. Draw balconies on construction paper and cut them out.

7. Glue the balconies to the house and cover with paper strips, leaving the tops open.

8. Paint the house. Draw windows and a door with a pencil.

9. Add details as you paint the roof, door, and windows.

💡 *Use your imagi-nation:* You can make a collection of other buildings of all shapes and sizes. Create a whole city, a small town, or a farm!

Nutty Neckties

☞ YOU'LL NEED: newspaper, glue, water, cardboard, stickers, paint, a stapler, pictures from magazines or wrapping paper, an elastic band, and scissors.

1. Draw a tie on cardboard and cut it out.

2. Roll up paper to look like a knot and glue it to the top of the tie.

3. Wrap the tie with paper strips that are coated with glue on both sides.

4. After the paper strips are half dry, cover the tie with a wide strip of paper.

5. Staple an elastic band to the back of the tie.

6. Glue a folded strip of paper to the back of the tie to hide the staples.

7. When the tie dries, paint it. Add designs to the tie if you like.

Happy-Hair Headbands

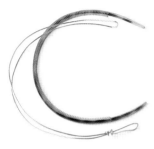

1. Bend two lengths of wire into a semicircle.

2. Fold two sheets of newspaper accordion-style.

☞ **YOU'LL NEED:** *newspaper, glue, water, wire, masking tape, paints, a paintbrush, shells, and scissors.*

3. Twist two strips around the wire. Start at the ends of the wire and work toward the center.

4. Wrap the band with masking tape to hold the paper in place.

5. Cover the band with two layers of wet paper strips that are coated with glue on both sides.

6. Once the band dries, paint it. You can glue shells to the band for decoration.

7. To make ladybugs, roll little balls of paper. Glue them to the headband, cover them with paper strips, and paint them.

💡 *Use your imagination:*
Try making flowers, spiders, planets, or tiny fruits.

A Ghostly Game

1. Mark the outline of a shoebox on a large piece of cardboard. Draw the shape of a ghost around it. In the center, draw a circle.

☛ *YOU'LL NEED: a shoebox, newspaper, glue, water, scissors, cardboard, a marker, cellophane paper, paint, and a paintbrush.*

2. Cut out the ghost and the circle. Hint: It's easiest to cut out the circle if you start at the center and cut out triangles.

3. Glue the hollow end of the shoebox where you marked its outline. Fold the base of the ghost outward so it can stand up.

4. To make hair, roll up and twist two sheets of newspaper. Roll up a third sheet and fold it in half. For the eyes, make two circles out of crinkled paper.

5. Cover the fingers with strips of glued paper.

6. Glue the rolled sheets and the eyes to the cardboard.

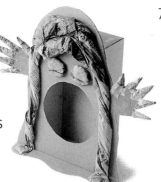

7. Cover the entire ghost sculpture with two layers of wet paper strips that are coated with glue on both sides.

8. When the paper dries, paint the inside and the outside of the box.

9. For the playing pieces, make balls out of crinkled white paper covered with different colors of cellophane paper. Glue the ends of the cellophane.

10. Paint the nails, eyes, hair, and wrinkles. Bet you can't even get one ball in!

💡 **Use your imagination:**
Instead of cutting a circle for a mouth, try other shapes or cut out the eyes of your creature instead!

Clever Clips and Pins

☛ *YOU'LL NEED: paper pulp, paint, a paintbrush, bobby pins, safety pins, strips of cotton or gauze, and a toothpick.*

1. To make a sneaker, create a ball from paper pulp, roll it out, and form an indent in one end with your finger. Make a very thin roll for a shoelace, shape it into a bow, and place it on the shoe. When the sneaker dries, paint it any color you like.

2. To make a chocolate cookie, form a paper pulp ball, flatten it, and stretch it out a little. Use a toothpick to press indents on one side. You can paint the cookie when it dries.

3. To make a telephone, form a roll and shape it by squeezing it a little in the center. Paint it after it dries.

4. To make a book, form a ball, flatten it, and shape it into a rectangle. Make a slight indent down the center. When the book is dry, paint the pages white and the words black.

5. Attach a bobby pin or a safety pin to the back of each piece, using strips of cotton or gauze that have been dipped in glue. To glue the bobby pin, separate its prongs with a toothpick.

💡 **Use your imagination:** *You can make a collection of just about anything. With basic shapes, such as circles and oblongs, you can make anything from bugs to bottles, or footballs to frankfurters!*

6. Now admire, and wear, the first four pieces of your clever collection!

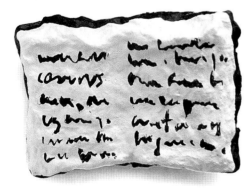

Rovin' Robot

☛ YOU'LL NEED: newspaper, glue, water, scissors, a large and a small matchbox, a toilet paper tube, ribbon, bendable straws, foil cups, colored tacks, and adhesive tape.

1. Glue a small matchbox to a larger one.

2. Flatten a toilet paper tube. Cut it so that it's a little wider than the larger matchbox. Glue the larger piece to the matchbox, as shown.

3. Crinkle a sheet of newspaper and insert it in the tube.

4. Make two holes in the sides of the larger box. Cut two bendable straws and glue them in the holes.

18

5. Cover the figure with wet paper strips that are coated with glue on both sides. Use vertical strips for the first layer. Add horizontal strips for the second layer. Wind narrow strips around the arms.

6. Apply two more layers of paper strips.

7. When the newspaper is dry, paint your robot.

8. Cut off the sides of foil cups and use them to dress up your robot. You can also decorate it with colored tacks, or stickers, and adhesive tape. Now program your robot and give him his first command!

💡 *Use your imagination:*
You can create a whole collection of aliens or androids, each with different controls and different abilities!

19

Moustache Mask

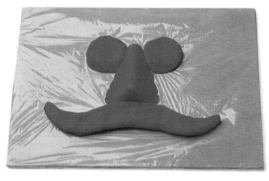

☛ **YOU'LL NEED: newspaper, glue, water, scissors, plastic wrap, ribbon, a sheet of cardboard or wood, modeling clay, liquid soap, paint, and a paintbrush.**

1. Make a cylinder, a cone, and two balls out of modeling clay, as shown.

2. Cover a flat base, such as cardboard, with plastic wrap. Place the shapes on it to form two eyes, a nose, and a large moustache.

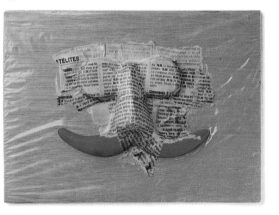

3. Join the pieces together, smooth them out, and coat the shape with liquid soap.

4. Cover it with wet newspaper strips that are coated with glue. Apply four layers.

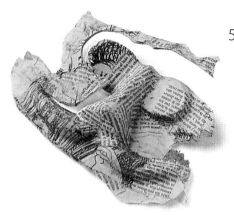

5. When the mask dries, remove it from the mold and cut away any excess paper.

6. Paint the eyes and the nose.

7. Next, paint the moustache and the pupils of the eyes.

8. Make holes in the pupils and nose. Glue ribbons to the back of the mask on both sides. Put on your mask! You've certainly grown quite a moustache!

💡 **Use your imagination:** *Make whiskers where the moustache was and you can be a cat, tiger, or lion. Make tusks instead and you can be an elephant or a walrus!*

Funtastic Footprints

1. Try making footprints from paper pulp. To make fox prints, form a ball out of paper pulp and flatten it. Mark the paw prints with the cap of a ballpoint pen. Remove excess pulp with a spatula and mark the claws with a toothpick. Make three more prints the same way.

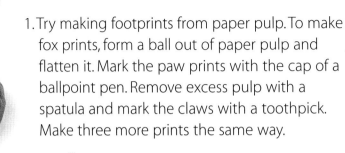

2. For human prints, make a ball out of paper pulp. Flatten and lengthen it. Mark the toes with the cap of a ballpoint pen and hollow out the rest of the print with your finger. Use a spatula to cut off excess pulp. Do the same for the other foot.

☛ **YOU'LL NEED: paper pulp, glue, paint, scissors, a ballpoint pen cap, a spatula, a toothpick, and small magnets.**

3. After the footprints dry, paint them. Glue small magnets to the back of each one and have them "walk" across your refrigerator!

A House Mouse

☛ **YOU'LL NEED: paper pulp, glue, scissors, a toothpick, pipe cleaners, broom bristles, black construction paper, a pencil, paints, a paintbrush, and double-sided adhesive tape.**

1. Flatten a ball of paper pulp and form it into a mouse. Make the ears out of two flattened little balls.

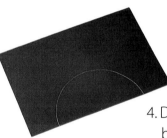

2. Use a toothpick to make small holes for whiskers and a larger hole for the tail. Let it dry.

3. Make the tail out of a piece of pipe cleaner. Use broom bristles for the whiskers.

4. Draw a semicircle on black construction paper and cut it out.

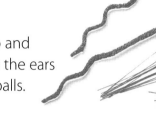

5. Glue on the whiskers and tail. Paint the ears, nose, and eye.

6. Stick double-sided adhesive tape to the back of the mouse and to the semicircle.

7. Place that pesky mouse against a wall in your room, and watch your cat go crazy!

23

Peeking Person

☞ YOU'LL NEED: newspaper, glue, water, scissors, cardboard, paint, a paintbrush, an old toothbrush, and double-sided adhesive tape.

1. On cardboard, draw the outline of a head with its hair on end. Draw two hands, as shown. Cut the shapes out carefully.

2. Roll up sheets of newspaper for the hair. Roll and cut another sheet for the four fingers of each hand. Fold paper to make two circles for the eyes.

3. Glue all the paper pieces to the cardboard, as shown.

24

4. Cover the head and hands with layers of paper strips coated with glue on both sides.

5. Once the pieces are dry, paint the face, eyes, and hands.

6. Cover the face area with paper. Paint the hair. Then dip an old toothbrush in black paint and run a spatula through the bristles to sprinkle paint on the hair. Remove the paper on the face and paint the details of the eyes and the eyebrows.

7. Stick double-sided adhesive tape to the back of the three pieces and place them on the frame of a door, window, or picture!

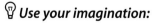

💡 *Use your imagination:*
How about making your pet or a favorite wild animal? Instead of spiky hair, you can do long donkey or rabbit ears, antennae, or even a crown!

Hangers with Heart

1. To make a skull, form a ball out of paper pulp and place it on the neck of a hanger. When it's partly dry, shape the jawbone and make openings for the eyes and nose. When the skull is dry, paint it with fluorescent colors.

☞ **YOU'LL NEED: paper pulp, glue, scissors, hangers, fluorescent paint, and a paintbrush.**

2. To make mushrooms, shape a circle and a roll of paper pulp and place them around the neck of a hanger. When it's partially dry, add pulp to form the large and small mushrooms. When the mushrooms are dry, paint the caps and add dots.

3. To make a snake, form a long role and wrap it around the neck of a hanger. Let it dry halfway before you finish shaping the snake. Once it's dry, paint it. Apply the base paint first. Then paint the spots and the eyes.

4. To make a monkey, form a ball of paper pulp, lengthen it a little, and shape the head. Form four separate rolls, two for the arms and two for the legs. When it's partly dry, add the ears and the tail. Paint the monkey when it's dry.

💡 *Use your imagination:*
You can add almost anything to your hanger collection. Try doing food, flowers, insects, or other animals.

Money Melon Bank ✂

☞ YOU'LL NEED: newspaper, glue, water, scissors, a pencil, a bowl, liquid soap, construction paper, paint, and a paintbrush.

1. Coat the inside of a glass bowl with liquid soap. Cover it with four layers of crisscrossed strips of newspaper that are coated with glue.

2. When the paper dries, carefully remove the bowl.

3. Cut off any excess paper.

4. Trace the rim of the bowl on construction paper, and cut out the circle.

28

5. Glue the circle to the rim of the paper bowl.

6. Cover the lid with strips of wet newspaper coated with glue.

7. When it's dry, paint a white band around the edge of the top and paint the outside green.

8. Paint the watermelon pulp red and the seeds black.

9. Ask an adult to cut a slot in the center of the top for the fruitiest bank in the neighborhood!

💡 **Use your imagination:** *Try other fruits, such as an orange, a kiwi, or an apple for your bank. Or add a handful of rice before you close the top to make a nifty instrument!*

How to Work with Paper Strips

☛ *YOU'LL NEED: liquid soap, newspaper and white glue diluted with water (one tablespoon of water for every tablespoon of glue).*

1. Fill a container with water. Place a sheet of newspaper in the water and let it soak for three minutes.

2. Carefully remove the sheet and spread it on a table covered with dry newspaper.

3. Use a brush to apply a coat of glue.

4. With your hands, tear strips of paper, following the direction of the print.

5. When lining a mold, press the strips with a brush or your fingers so that bubbles don't form.

6. For the first layer, apply glue to the top of the strips. For the remaining layers, apply glue to the underside of the strips.

7. Apply a coat of glue between layers and to the final layer.

8. If you can, use different colors of newspaper from layer to layer. This way, you'll know where you've placed a layer and where you haven't.

9. For the best results, apply at least four layers of strips. They'll take about two days to dry. Use acrylic paints to paint papier-mâché.

Molds: You can use plates, plastic food containers, bowls—or your can make forms yourself with modeling clay. Before applying the paper strips, waterproof the mold by covering it with plastic wrap or brushing on a coat of concentrated liquid soap.

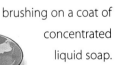

Bases: Use disposable materials like empty boxes, toilet paper tubes, and kitchen towel tubes.

How to Make Paper Pulp

☛ **YOU'LL NEED: narrow strips of newspaper, water, and white glue.**

1. Tear a newspaper into narrow strips.

2. Cut the newspaper strips into little pieces.

3. Cover the pieces with hot water. Let the paper soak for 24 hours.

4. Mash the pulp with a food beater, leaving it somewhat liquid. Then strain it.

5. Add a tablespoon of glue for each double sheet of newspaper you used. Knead it with your hands.

6. Strain it again. Squeeze it with your hands until you have a paste.

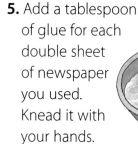

8. Wait for paper pulp to dry completely before painting it or gluing anything to it. If you paint it, use acrylic paints. In general, paper pulp takes three days to dry.

7. Work the paper pulp with your hands, modeling and rolling it carefully. Use a spatula or toothpicks to cut it.

WHERE TO GET SUPPLIES

Art & Woodcrafters Supply, Inc.
www.artwoodcrafter.com
Order a catalog or browse online for many different craft supplies.

Craft Supplies
www.craftsfaironline.com/Supplies.html
Features many different sites, each featuring products for specific hobbies.

Darice, Inc.
21160 Drake Road
Strongsville, OH 44136-6699
www.darice.com
Order a catalog or browse online for many different craft supplies.

Making Friends
www.makingfriends.com
Offers many kits and products for children's crafts.

National Artcraft
7996 Darrow Road
Twinsburg, OH 44087
www.nationalartcraft.com
This craft store features many products available through its catalog or online.

FOR MORE INFORMATION

Books

Chapman, Gillian. *Art From Fabric: With Projects Using Rags, Old Clothes, and Remnants.* New York, NY: Thomson Learning, 1995.

Chapman, Gillian. *Autumn* (Seasonal Crafts). Chatham, NJ: Raintree/Steck Vaughn, 1997.

Connor, Nikki. *Cardboard Boxes* (Creating Crafts From). Providence, RI: Copper Beech Books, 1996.

Gordon, Lynn. *52 Great Art Projects For Kids.* San Francisco, CA: Chronicle Books, 1996.

King, Penny. *Animals* (Artists' Workshop). New York, NY: Crabtree Publishing, 1996.

Newby, Nicole. *Cool Clay.* Mahwah, NJ: Troll, 1996.

Ross, Kathy. *The Best Holiday Crafts Ever.* Brookfield, CT: Millbrook Publishing, 1996.

Smith, Alistair. *Big Book of Papercraft.* Newton, MA: Educational Development Center, 1996.

Video

Blue's Clues Arts & Crafts. Nickelodeon. (1998).

Web Sites

Crafts For Kids
www.craftsforkids.miningco.com/mbody.htm
Many different arts and crafts activities are explained in detail.

Family Crafts
www.family.go.com
Search for crafts by age group. Projects include instructions, supply list, and helpful tips.

KinderCrafts
www.EnchantedLearning.com/Crafts
Step-by-step instructions explain how to make animal, dinosaur, box, and paper crafts, plus much more.

Making Friends
www.makingfriends.com
Contains hundreds of craft ideas with detailed instructions for children ages 2 to 12, including paper dolls, summer crafts, yucky stuff, and holiday crafts.

INDEX

Accessories
  Clever Clips and Pins, 16
  Happy-Hair Headbands, 13
  Nutty Neckties, 12
animals
  House Mouse, 23
  Slippery Snake, 4
  Terrific Pencil Toppers, 8

Cellophane paper, 14
Clever Clips and Pins, 16

cotton, 16
Funtastic Footprints, 22
Ghostly Game, 14
Hangers, 26
  Hangers with Heart, 26
Happy-Hair Headbands, 13
House Mouse, 23

Magnets
  Funtastic Footprints, 22
masks
  Moustache Mask, 20

Mini-Houses, 10
modeling clay, 20
Money Melon Bank, 28
Moustache Mask, 20
Nutty Neckties, 12
Peeking Person, 24
pencils, 8
people
  Peeking Person, 24
  Terrific Pencil Toppers, 8
pipe cleaners, 23

Ribbon, 18, 20
Rovin' Robot, 18
Slippery Snake, 4
stamps, 4
Star Cruiser, 6
stickers, 6, 12, 19
straws, 18
Terrific Pencil Toppers, 8
Wire, 4
wrapping paper, 12